To Dan
Best of luck!

ROBERT EARL KEEN

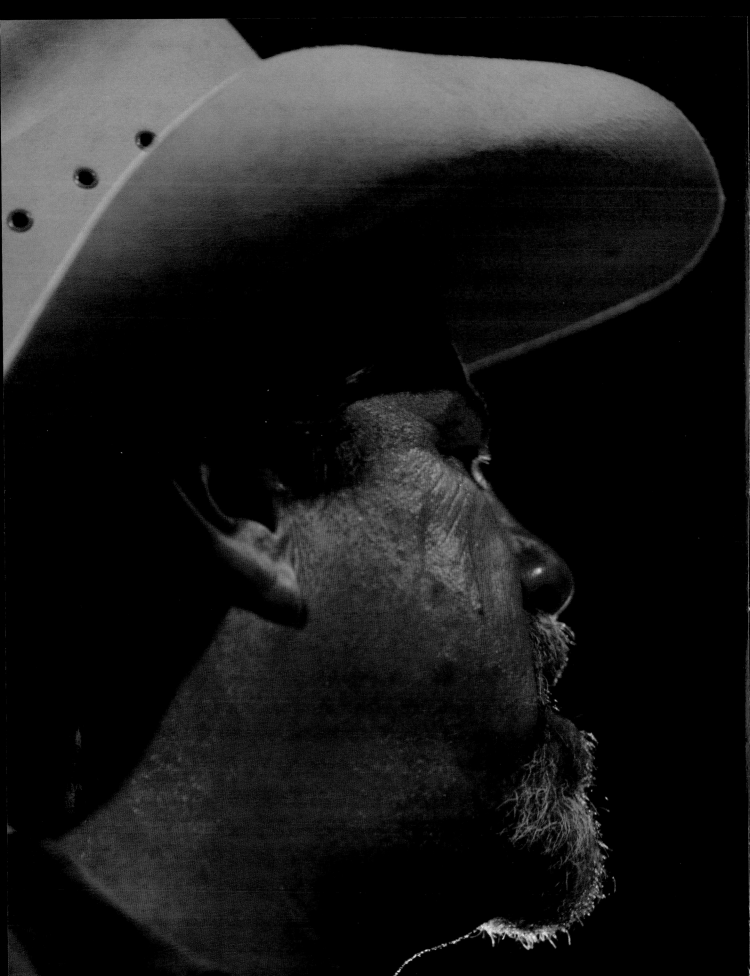

ROBERT EARL KEEN

THE ROAD GOES ON FOREVER AND THE MUSIC NEVER ENDS

UNIVERSITY OF TEXAS PRESS, AUSTIN

Brad and Michele Moore Roots Music Series

The paper used in this book meets the
minimum requirements of
ANSI/NISO Z39.48-1992 (R1997)
(Permanence of Paper).

ISBN: 978-0-292-71999-6

Library of Congress Control Number
2008936665

PHOTOGRAPHS BY: Lisa Krantz
(jacket, cover, end sheets, pp. 4, 10-11,
28-29, 42-43, 54-55, 70-71, 80-81,
90-91, 104-105, 116, 122-123)
DESIGN BY: EmDash LLC

HISTORICAL PHOTOGRAPHS BY:
Peter Figen, Glen Rose, Peter Moore
Allison Smith, C.P. Vaughn, Jeff Copp,
Merri Cyr, CUBS PHOTOGRAPHER: Steve Green,
Pat Johnson, Steve Green, Kathleen Keen

Some of the photos were taken
by family, friends and fans.

24 SONGS

ACKNOWLEDGMENTS

My sincerest thanks go to Melissa Story-Haycraft for getting everybody together and keeping this project rolling. Thanks to Dave Hamrick for his guidance and encouragement. Rich Brotherton not only plays beautiful guitar, but he can also write out what he plays in musical notation, and that's what he did. Thanks, Rich. When this book was no more than an concept, Caryne Prater's ideas showed us what it might become. Erin Mayes and Kate Iltis of EmDash designed a wonderful book. Thanks to the other band guys, Bill, Tom, Marty, and Danny, for bringing these songs to life. Cindy Howell keeps us on the road and me on the straight and narrow. Thank you.

None of what a musician does could be accomplished without the support of a loving family. Mine is the best. Kathleen, Clara, and Chloe are my inspiration. Thank you.

I never imagined having a songbook;

however, when someone suggested I do one, I thought, "why not?" The first book was easy because I simply took all the songs I had written up to that point and, with the help of my wife, Kathleen, added some nifty photos and presto.

This book was more challenging. I have boxes of songs. I wanted to include songs that I know people like, but I have personal favorites that don't always crossover. They have to be good songs. How do you decide that? The incomparable Dave Hickey says a good song is "one that tastes good in your mouth when you sing it and feels good under your boot when you tap it out."

Stop the search. Look no further. I think these meet the criteria.

"If you could describe
the perfect homecoming.
This is mine."

FEELIN' GOOD AGAIN
Walking Distance | 1998

FEELIN' GOOD AGAIN

Standin' down on Main Street across from Mister Blue's
In my faded leather jacket and my weathered Brogan shoes.
A chill north wind was blowin' but the spring was comin' on
As I wondered to myself just how long I had been gone.
So I strolled across old Main Street, walked down a flight of stairs,
Stepped into the hall and saw all my friends were there.
A neon sign was flashin' "Welcome, come on in."
It feels so good feelin' good again.

My favorite band was playin' an Otis Redding song.
When they sang the chorus everybody sang along.
Dan and Margarita were swayin' side by side.
I heard they were divorcin' but I guess they let it slide.
And I wished I had some money with which to buy a round.
I wished I'd cashed my paycheck before I came to town.
But I reached into my pocket, found three twenties and a ten.
It feels so good feelin' good again.

There was old man Perkins sittin' on his stool
watchin' Butch and Jimmy John talkin' loud and playin' pool.
The boys from Silver City were standin' by the fire
Singin' like they thought they were the Tabernacle choir.
And I wanted you to see 'em all, I wished that you were there.
I looked across the room and saw you standin' on the stair,
and when I caught your eye I saw you break into a grin.
It feels so good feelin' good again.

It feels so good feelin' good again.

A steady hand and a determined gaze net 5-year-old Will Grote the thrill of victory at the pop gun booth. The young Bryan cowboy chose an American flag as his prize. Another cowboy having a good time whooping it up is Robert Keen of the Front Porch Boys.

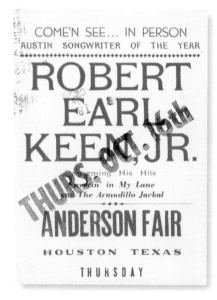

"I was writing songs for Gringo Honeymoon. It was Christmas time and I realized not one of the Holiday songs remotely reflected my Christmas experiences. So I wrote one."

MERRY CHRISTMAS FROM THE FAMILY

Gringo Honeymoon | 1994

MOM GOT DRUNK AND DAD GOT DRUNK AT OUR CHRISTMAS PARTY

WE WERE DRINKIN' CHAMPAYNE PUNCH AND HOMEMADE EGG NOG

LITTLE SISTER BROUGHT HE NEW BOYFRIEND HE WAS A MEXICAN

WE DIDN'T KNOW WHAT TO THINK OF HIM TIL HE SANG FELIZ NAVIDAD

FELIZ NAVIDAD ... FELIZ NAVIDAD

BROTHER KEN BROUGHT HIS KIDS W/HIM THE THREE FROM HIS 1ST WIFE LYNN

AND THE TWO IDENTICAL TWINS FROM HIS SECOND WIFE MARY. NEL

OF COURSE HE BROUGHT HIS NEW BRIDE KAY WHO TALKS ALL ABOUT AA

CHAIN SMOKIN' WHILE THE STEREO PLAYS NOEL, NOEL.

THE FIRST NOEL ...

CHORUS: CARVE THE TURKEY TURN THE BALL GAME ON

MAKE MARGARITAS WHEN THE EGG NOG'S GONE

SEND SOMEBODY TO THE QUICK PAC STORE

WE NEED SOME ICE AND AN EXTENTION CHORD,

A CAN OF BEAN DIP AND SOME DIET RIGHT'S,

A BOX OF TAMPONS AND SOME MARLBORO LIGHTS

HALLELUJIAH EVERYBODY SAY CHEESE

MERRY CHRISTMAS FROM THE FAMILY

FRAN & RITA DROVE FROM HARLINGEN I DON'T REMEMBER HOW I'M KIN TO THEM

BUT WHEN THEY TRIED TO PLUG THEIR MOTORHOME IN THE BLEW OUR CHRISTMAS LIGHTS

COUSIN DAVID KNEW JUST WHAT WENT WRONG HE STOOD AND WAITED OUT ON OUR FRONT LAWN

HE THROUGH THE BREAKER AND THE LIGHTS CAME ON WE SANG SILENT NIGHT

OH SILENT NIGHT

CARVE THE TURKEY TURN THE BALL GAME ON

MAKE BLOODY MARYS CAUSE WE ALL WANT ONE

SEND SOMEBODY TO THE STOP & GO

WE NEED SOME ~~BRAPAPOS~~ CELERY AND A CAN OF FAKE SNOW

A BAG OF FRITOS AND SOME DIET RIGHTS

A ~~PINT OF CHEESE WHIZ~~ BOX OF CRACKERS AND SOME SALEM LIGHTS

HALLELJIAH EVERYBODY SAY CHEESE

MERRY CHRISTMAS FROM THE FAMILY

"Arabian Nights meets the good, bad and the ugly."

THE TRAVELING STORM
What I Really Mean | 2005

THE TRAVELING STORM

In a year that is not now
From a place unknown
I travel on the mountain roads
Looking for someone.

Sewn inside my vest, a letter
Tells me where and when.
In my purse a sacred dagger.
On my horse I run.

Restless girl beside
The water, tending to a fire,
Kissed a boy and then another,
Suiting up for war.

Heard a broken band of
Gypsies singing ancient songs.
Gave all my silver to
A beggar, still he wanted more.

Oh, the town of stone
And timber. Celebration reigned.
No one there seems to
Remember why they carry on.

Crowded 'round a man of
Marble speaking foreign tongue,
There the stone began to
Crumble, and the crowd did moan.

In the unforgiving morning
Caravans of shame
Turn south to the dry land
Highway; I turn to the sea.

Like a snake so quick and
Deadly, sleepless, coiled and cool,
The one I seek is making
Ready, waiting patiently.

Pity not the weary traveler,
He lives in his mind.
He is friend of wind and
Weather and from fire is born.

Pity then the cool betrayer waiting patiently.
No precaution made will save him from the
Traveling storm.

Battalion photo by Lynn Blan

Studying? No …

Robert Keen portrays Death in the "Death Knocks" segment of a Reader's Theatre adaptation of Woody Allen's "Getting Even." Keen and four other students presented their interpretation of four of Allen's works in Rudder Forum Tuesday evening. The oral interpretation group is part of speech communication at Texas A&M University.

approx 1 min.
margo 35 sec

	Song	Grade	
3:30	THINK IT OVER	D	
3:59	4th of July	B	fiddle good - (starts before Rudeman on other AC1)
4:32 1	Sunday	B+	Be sure - cut the pattern
5:15	Levelland	D	
2:46 2	Aman Holiday	B+	fiddle all in unison - Start harmony @ end off. to fit lessen richis vocals?
5:35	OH. Rosie	no grade	

Intro Of Band is good - — how long does this take -
doesn't much good TV
Hair don't Just Margo's intro — with "We had much problem — go into Son of Bro?

3:55 √	I. Wonder	D	
3:26 3.	Son of Brother	B	
3:40 4	Then Came LoMein	B	guitar a little loud - Guet around Response
3:36 5	Undon	B+	
+18 6.	Waterfall	B+	Vocals? mandoln solo?
4:39	Raton		

If we have to cut to 5 can we bring margo on w/Caroline

Can we leave the last intro?

"True? Yes, unfortunately."

CORPUS CHRISTI BAY

A Bigger Piece of Sky | 1993

CORPUS CHRISTI BAY

I worked the rigs from three to midnight on the Corpus Christi Bay.
I'd get off and drink 'till daylight, sleep the morning away.
I had a plan to take my wages, leave all the rigs behind for good,
But that life it is contagious and it gets down in your blood.

I lived in Corpus with my brother. We were always on the run.
We were bad for one another but we were good at having fun.
We got stoned along the sea wall. We got drunk and rolled a car.
We knew the girls at every dance hall, had a tab at every bar.

CHORUS

If I could live my life all over it wouldn't matter anyway
'Cause I never could stay sober on the Corpus Christi Bay.
On the Corpus Christi Bay.
If I could live my life all over it wouldn't matter anyway
'Cause I never could stay sober on the Corpus Christi Bay.

CHORUS

My brother had a wife and family. You know he gave 'em a good home.
But his wife thought we were crazy, and one day we found her gone.
We threw her clothes into the car trunk, her photographs, her rosary.
We went to the pier and got drunk; threw it all into the sea.

CHORUS

Now my brother lives in Houston. He married for a second time.
He got a good job with the union and it's keepin' him in line.
He came to Corpus just this weekend. Man, it was good to see him here.
He said he finally gave up drinkin', then he ordered me a beer.

CHORUS

CHORUS

July 5, 1983

Dear Dan,

I don't remember when I wrote you before, but I do remember asking you for money. I know you probably think this is a sorry way to go about getting an album, but to tell the truth it is only an investment. I've got a list of twenty people (family, friends, ex-employers) who I thought might like to chip in $100.00 each so they can have their very own ROBERT KEEN album. Lucky you you were one of the twenty.

All seriousness aside, I want to get this under way by Aug 1st, so if you feel so inclined, do so. If not I've got some pretty lude color photos of you that will be used against you. Only kidding! Check it out!

Love, Robert

"Old outlaws never die,
they just run out of bullets."

PAINT THE TOWN BEIGE
A Bigger Piece of Sky | 1993

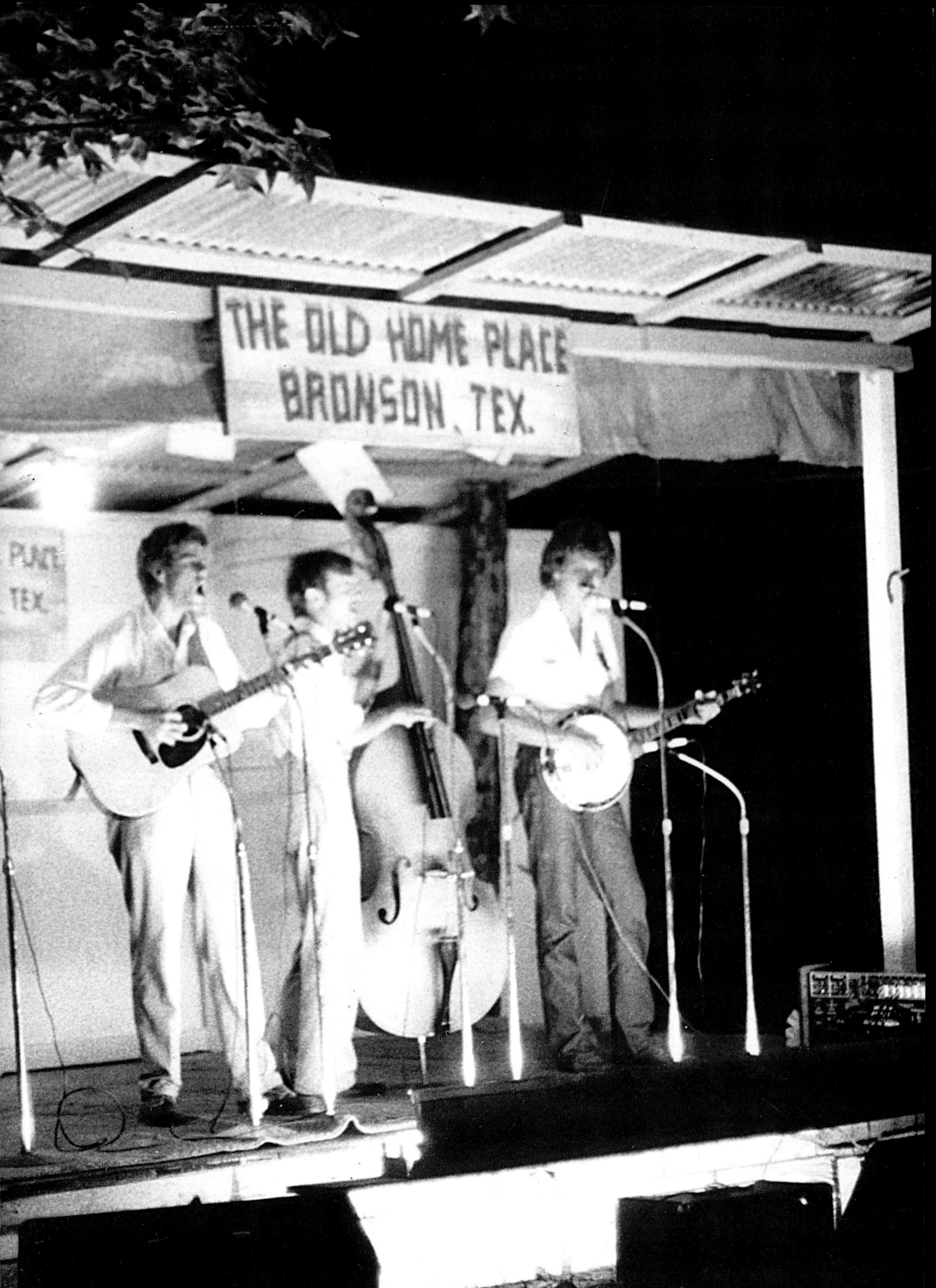
THE OLD HOME PLACE
BRONSON, TEX.

PAINT THE TOWN BEIGE

I gave up the fast lane for a blacktop country road.
Just burned out on all that talk about the motherlode.
I traded for a songbird, a bigger piece of sky.
When I miss the good old days I can't imagine why.

CHORUS

Still I get restless and drive into town.
I cruise once down Main Street and turn back around.
It's crazy but God knows I don't act my age
Like an old desperado who paints the town beige.
I gave up the fast lane.

Down along the river and past the swimming hole
You can find your peace of mind with just a fishin' pole.
And you can walk the river for miles and miles on end
And never stop believin' in that dream around the bend.

CHORUS

Still I get restless and drive into town.
My radio playin' my window rolled down.
It's crazy but God knows I don't act my age
Like an old desperado who paints the town beige.
I gave up the fast lane.

Deep down in the winter, time slows to a crawl.
There's really nothin' much to do until the first spring thaw.
It's then I get to thinkin' I must have gone insane.
Memories roll through my mind like a long, slow railroad train.

CHORUS

Still I get restless and drive into town.
Watch the world through a windshield as it all comes unwound.
It's crazy but God knows I don't act my age
Like an old desperado who paints the town beige.
I gave up the fast lane.

"Praise the mighty onion.
Do not be Alarmed!"

FARM FRESH ONIONS

Farm Fresh Onions | 2003

Keen writes songs for people, not radio execs

8099T

**By Paulette Flowers
and Otto Kitsinger**

ROBERT EARL Keen once said, "I wish I could write 'normal.' I would like to be more mainstream. I try, but I can't pull it off."

Which is why you may not be familiar with Robert Earl's music. "Normal" in this context means radio friendly. It means sounding like everybody else. It means writing songs that 24-year-old marketing experts think the 18 to 24 year-old "target demographic" will like.

Robert Earl writes songs that are as long as they need to be, instead of writing with a timer set to go off at the three-minute mark, the "radio-friendly" length. His songs aren't pretty, either. But they are true and funny and honest.

His funny songs, like "Five Pound Bass" or "Merry Christmas from the Family," make you wonder where he met your uncle and who invited Robert Earl to your last family Christmas gathering. Other songs, like "Mariano" and "The Road Goes on Forever," are the works of a master storyteller who understands the saying "God is in the details."

"MARIANO," for instance, portrays an illegal immigrant gardener who is eventually deported. But Robert Earl's song doesn't insult this dignified man with unwanted pity. Instead, he gives a crystal clear picture of a real man he once knew who, after working all day "like a piston in an engine," is "sitting on a stone in a southeasterly direction" thinking of "the folks he calls his own."

Catfood blue Purina
Tangled up in Blue

Robert Earl Keen
I'm Fresh Onions

Hey! Wear a John Deere Cap!
The real symbol of America!

Farm Fresh Onions

Truth is all I'm looking for
Town to town and door to door
Happiness is nothing more
than Sunday at the zoo
Riding high inside the wires
the ~~sun~~ sum of all of my desires
Earth & rain all it requires
is love from me and you

Big & round and sweet and real   and then appear
good to eat and fun to steal ——— to anyone who
a half a pound will make a meal   wants a meal
that's sure to fortify
Kiss the stars & sweat the years
it appears that all your fears (happen
won't bring to life those honest tears
that feel so good to cry.

People walking everywhere planes are falling from the air
Take a good look in the mirror mirror on the wall
Overwhelming to the mind too confused but still undecided
to stay the course until I find the onion in us all

Thinking straight into the sun where
Where at its core the onion one
wants you to know there's never none
there's no need for alarm
Where Millions Billions zillions wait
proliferate their blissful state
to welcome your arrival date
The day you buy the farm

"Who else would I be here for?"

I'LL BE HERE FOR YOU
Walking Distance | 1998

I'LL BE HERE FOR YOU

Good times come and then they go.
The rain will fall, the wind will blow.
Through it all you gotta know
I'll do what I can do to protect you
Right or wrong,
Heal the hurt 'til the hurt is gone.
I'll be right where I belong.
I'll be here for you.

CHORUS

I'll be here when the sky turns gray,
The sun goes blind and the moon won't stay.
I'll be the light to guide your way
Onto some place new.
I'll be here when the crowd is gone,
The last note fades on the very last song.
I'll be the road you take home.
I'll be here for you.

CHORUS

When your star falls from the sky
And your wings don't want to fly,
Just remember I'm standing by
To help to see you through.
'Cause better days will come again,
Clouds will break, your heart will mend.
I'll be where I've always been;
I'll be here for you.

CHORUS

"I've lived in small towns
long enough to write
about them. All true."

WILD WIND
Gravitational Forces | 2001

ROBERT
EARL
KEEN, JR.

MARCH

2nd *The Cactus Cafe UT Campus* 9:30 - 12:00
3rd *The Cactus Cafe UT Campus* 9:30 Open
6th-10th *Filling Station* 9:30 - 1:00
11th *Gruene Hall, Gruene Tex.,* 4:00 - 8:00
15th & 16th *Cherokee Station, Temple Tx.* 8:00 - 12:00
22nd & 23rd *Guns, San Marcos, Tx.,* 9:00 - 12:00
APRIL 6th   9 PM
MY ALBUM PARTY
@ Butch Hancock's Dixie Bar & Bustop
900 E. 5th *next to* I 35

WILD WIND

Down on Main Street after sundown
Goodtime Charlie and Wanderin' Bill
Thought they might hold up Hoppy's Drive-In.
One got away and one never will.

CHORUS

That's the way it goes around here.
I think everybody knows.
That's the song they've been singin' for years.
That's the way the wild wind blows.

Too tall Annie kept her money
In a Bible she never read.
They found Lefty, her first ex-husband,
In his new pickup truck
At the bottom of the riverbed.

CHORUS

Luther Martin, he ain't got nobody,
But he sells papers and buys his wine.
His granddaddy owned half of Main Street.
Luther's daddy didn't have a dime.

CHORUS

Ain't no secret old Doc Skinner
Wrote prescriptions and made lots of friends.
He could dance like nobody's business.
Folks around here are sure missing him.

CHORUS

"If you've had a horse,
you've had a sorry one.
This is your story too."

THAT BUCKIN' SONG
Walking Distance | 1998

THAT BUCKIN' SONG

I had a horse named - Bad Luck.
She weren't good lookin' but she sure could buck

CHORUS
Yahoo hey hey! Yippee yi cy yey!

I put my mama on her, she threw her in the air.
My mama said, "Son, that's a mother-buckin' mare."

CHORUS

Took her to the rodeo, she won second place,
She was really buckin' good in the buckin' barrel race

CHORUS

She won a thousand dollars, I put it in my hat.
Bought a brand new saddle, she bucked me out of that.

CHORUS

She bucked me on the pick-up truck, she bucked me on the fence.
My daddy said, "Son, you got no buckin' sense."

CHORUS

So if you got a bucker don't ever buck around.
That buckin' mother bucker will buck you on the ground.

CHORUS

"My last day in
Nashville, Tennessee."

THEN CAME LO MEIN
Picnic | 1997

Unconventional the rule for Keen

By Butch Hause
Special to The Denver Post

Robert Earl Keen is not your average Texas songwriter.

"I'm not really sure where I fit," Keen said, taking a break from a Nashville recording session. "Some people hear my stuff and think I'm a joke. I guess I do write some pretty strange stuff sometimes, but people who know me know where I'm coming from."

Keen, who plays the Mercury Cafe tomorrow night, is no joke in the songwriting field. Although he hasn't written a No. 1 hit, his music has been recorded by such diverse talents as Nanci Griffith, Joe Ely, Eddy Raven and Kelly Willis. He was a staff writer for MCA/Nashville for several years, but he tired of their safe, "middle-of-the-road" attitude.

"As far as MCA was concerned, you were out on a limb if you used a word with more than

three syllables," Keen said.

Lyrically, he's humorous, oblique and never conventional. And although he's been identified with Austin's "alternative" country writers, like Townes Van Zandt and Guy Clark, Keen's music leaves plenty of room for a new category.

His twisted outlook on life couldn't have been predicted from his formative years. Raised in Houston, he attended high school, played a little bluegrass music and fished for bass. Enrolling at Texas A&M, Keen looked at his strengths and focused his studies accordingly.

"I defied 'Aggie' tradition and majored in English," Keen said,

as he explained with more than a little levity. "I figured hey, I can speak English. I should be able to handle this."

At A&M he met another displaced student — a journalism major with a gift for music.

"Lyle Lovett was as out of place at that school as I was," Keen recalled, "so we ended up rooming together." They wrote and performed together, too.

The relationship yielded several musical gems, including "This Old Porch," which appeared on Lovett's first album.

Comfortable and confident about his songs, Keen has no delusions of hit records or major concert tours, at least not yet.

"You've got to be on the radio," Keen said. "Right now, radio is that maple syrup baritone singer thing. I've got the baritone, but I think it's more like gasoline than maple syrup. That might take some getting used to."

THEN CAME LO MEIN

There were lean times, they were tough.
There were mean times they were rough,
And the good times didn't outweigh the bad.
I was sad you were bitter but you were no quitter
When nothin' was all that we had.

We were drinkin' a lot.
We were thinkin' of tyin' the knot
Or maybe throw in the towel.
Make up have a kid. Break up and we did
But only just for a while.

Then came lo mein and going insane
At the Chinese cafe way downtown.
I was steamed, I was fried but you stood by my side
When I had my nervous breakdown.

There were noodles galore
All over the floor
And hot mustard sauce everywhere.
I held your hand 'til you calmed down again,
And picked out the rice in your hair.

After that we agreed
When in fact what we need
Is to pack up and take the first plane.
Take a bus, take a bike,
Take care, take a hike,
Take out but leave the lo mein

I remember it now when we order kung pao
And bow our heads to say grace
The day we left town and that nervous breakdown
At the all-you-can-eat Chinese place,
At the Chinese café way downtown.

Official
Program
$1

2nd Annual

WILLIE NELSON

4th of July
Picnic

College Station,
Texas

July 4, 5 & 6, 1974

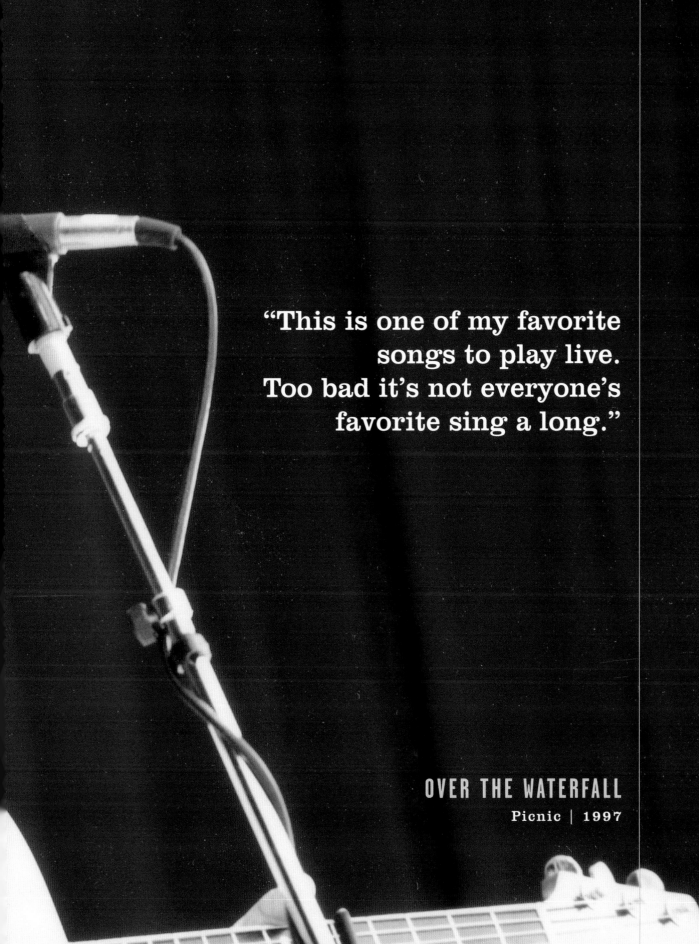

"This is one of my favorite songs to play live. Too bad it's not everyone's favorite sing a long."

OVER THE WATERFALL
Picnic | 1997

OVER THE WATERFALL

I slipped through your fingers into the clouds,
Ran down the concrete hallways,
Pushed through the crowds.
I watched by the water, reached for the sun.
Why did I bother? What's done is done.

CHORUS

And all that's left of me now is waiting to drown.
Over the waterfall (fallin' down),
Over the waterfall (fallin' down),
Over the waterfall (fallin' down), I fall down.

Soldiers of fortune stand by your door.
You can't remember what you hired them for.
You cleared your conscience and I left a stain.
The beauty of sadness is feeling the pain.

CHORUS

BRIDGE

And only the sad stone man can hear my cry
And only the tall blue girl can see.
I lost my way, I left no alibi,
So no one will know you knew me.

Randomly speaking, pieces of light.
The clowns from the circus got drunk here last night.
They talked of reunion then left on their own.
What they've never known
Is what you've always known.

CHORUS

Songwriters to entertain in Aspen

ASPEN - Three of Texas' best known songwriters will meet at the Wheeler Opera House Aug. 28 for a triple-header acoustic concert billed as an intimate journey deep into the heart and soul of Texas.

Guy Clark, Townes Van Zandt and Robert Earl Keen Jr. are indivdually responsible for such classics as "Pancho and Lefty," "L.A. Freeway," and "If I Needed You" for country stars as diverse as Ricky Skaggs, Jerry Jeff Walker, Willie Nelson, Lyle Lovett and Nancy Griffith.

Each will play a solo set followed by a three-way, center stage country/folk jam.

The concert is a benefit for public access radio station KDNK. Reserved seat tickets are $14 for KDNK members, and $16 for non-members and are available at the Wheeler Ticket Office, 925-2750, or at KDNK in Carbondale.

The concert is sponsored by Main Street Music in Aspen, Smith's Clothing and the Hotel Aspen, and is produced by Music Gumbo Productions.

Van Zandt is the old dog of the trio, with Keen as the young pup and Clark somewhere in the middle. All three write about love, life, mythical characters and themselves.

Guy Clark

Townes Van Zandt

Robert Earl Keen Jr.

"Write what you know about ... write with a pencil and a big eraser," Clark said in a 1989 interview with the Dallas Mornign News.

Clark helped establish Walker's career with "L.A. Freeway" and lately helped out new stars Foster and Lloyd with his "Fair Shake."

Clark's latest album is titled "Old Friends," a two-year effort that he recorded in his basement. Rolling Stone said the album "represents truths so obvious we can't help missing them - and we should be pleased Clark pointed them out

Keen has three albums under his belt and according to reviews, keeps getting stronger. One writer said about Keen's current release, West Textures, "Whether he's whimsical or serious, he comes across as a brilliant outsider."

Mountain Leisure   Glenwood Post

Friday, August 24, 1990

DON'T MISS
T H E
ROBERT
EARL
KEEN, JR.
SHOW

Join the mailing list...
Free membership to an
exclusive gang, uh club.
Please supply the information below
and return to Robert. Thank You!

Name

Address

City   State   Zip

① Learn how to read music.

② Take some guitar lessons

③ Quit smoking

④ I want to do something really nice for my sister

⑤ Send everybody ~~*****~~ that I know
(and know there birthday) $5 on their birthday

⑥ Start and stick to a new running program

⑦ Quit dipping snuff

⑧ Floss

⑨ Create a solid stage image and stick to it.

⑩ Obtain some outside songs for our publishing company

⑪ Pay off our outstanding debts (Visa, Credit Cards,
Bank loan and Preston)

⑫ Make demos of all songs I write

⑬ Write a screen play

⑭ Complete the old car projects

⑮ Stop watching TV

⑯ Buy our building

⑰ Complete a new album

⑱ Take voice lessons and practice singing

⑲ Listen to more and wider variety of music

⑳ Be active in the community

㉑ Write my congressman and senator (state and national)

㉒ Make bookshelves and stereo cabinet for my room

㉓ Stand up for myself, my friends and my family

㉔ Write more letters to my friends and family

㉕ Always think and write songs

"What happens to you when everything goes wrong?"

NOT A DROP OF RAIN
Gravitational Forces | 2001

NOT A DROP OF RAIN

Streets are almost empty, shops are all closed down.
There's not a soul left in the bar to tell my troubles to.
Think I'll walk down to the river that runs just south of town.
I hate like hell when there ain't nothin' left to do
But stand beneath the river bridge and listen for the train.
It's been a long hot summer, not a drop of rain.

I broke down in December,
I headed for the coast.
I thought the wind and water would elevate my mind.
I surfaced in the springtime feelin' like a ghost,
Missin' more than ever the things I left behind.
Now I'm standin' on this riverbank and still cannot explain.
It's been a long hot summer, not a drop of rain.

My bag is full of letters unopened and unread.
I'm sure they'd tell the story of worry and of form.
My heart is beating heavy with all we left unsaid.
I swear to you I never meant you any harm.
But sacrifice and compromise could never stand the strain.
It's been a long hot summer, not a drop of rain.

Tonight I'll close my eyes again and try to see your face,
And Listen for your voice to tell me it's alright to sleep,
Convince myself I'll wake up in another time and place,
Knowin' all the while that it's a promise I can't keep.
A string of broken promises, another link of chain.
It's been a long hot summer, not a drop of rain.

The children on the playground, the lovers in the shade
Remind me of a life and time that feels more like a dream
When the sound of love and laughter was the music that we played
As we lay beside the waters of a never ending stream.
Now the stream has gone to hiding, the dream lives on in vain.
It's been a long hot summer, not a drop of rain.

The clouds are building slowly on the skyline to the east.
The wind and dust are dancing like the devil across the lake.
I could try to find a bottle or try to find a priest.
Salvation won't be traveling either road I take,
So I turn my collar to the wind that echoes this refrain.
It's been a long hot summer, not a drop of rain.

"If I were a cowboy
this would be my anthem."

NEW LIFE IN OLD MEXICO

Walking Distance | 1998

NEW LIFE IN OLD MEXICO

I crossed the Mississippi, turned south at San Antone.
A Bowie knife, a woolen coat, a grip bag on my arm.
It's all somebody needs to make it through the land.
Walk the night, travel light, cross the Rio Grande.
Someone strums a mandolin, soft gulf breezes blow.
My new life is waiting in old Mexico.

I was once a married man, livin' peacefully.
Hard to say exactly when the devil blinded me.
But there was some confusion when my sweet wife left this world.
Darker times, drunken crimes, a dead young working girl.
Left a jailer there in Caroline watching me from down below.
My new life is waiting in old Mexico.

BRIDGE

Livin' in the shadows, runnin' from my fame,
Blowin' where the wind blows, where no one knows my name.

In the El Vaquero Bar in the town of Eagle Pass,
Moments from my freedom, warm whiskey in my glass.
Some boracho took me for the man who stole his wife.
He went for his forty four as I reached for my knife.
He never fired a second shot. He was just too slow.
My new life is waiting in old Mexico.

I hear of hidden harbors south of Mazatlán
Where cool spring mountain waters meet the warm Pacific Sun.
I pray the miles I've traveled and all the sins I bear
Burn away like mornin' fog and vanish in the air.
Miles beyond the border now, many miles to go.
My new life is waiting in old Mexico.

"We played OKC the day after the bombing. The shock waves were felt for hundreds of miles."

SHADES OF GRAY
Picnic | 1997

WE MADE OKLAHOMA A LITTLE AFTER THREE
RANDY, HIS BROTHER BOB IN MY OLD GMC
WE HAD SOME MOONSHINE WHISKEY AND SOME OF BOB'S HOMEGROWN
WE WERE SO MESSED UP WE DIDN'T KNOW IF WE WERE DRUNK OR STONED

RANDY WAS A SAD SACK TALL & KINDA FRAIL
BOB WAS A RAVIN' MANIAC CRAZIER THAN HELL
THEY'D BEEN KICKED OUT OF HIGH SCHOOL A COUPLE YEARS AGO
FOR PUSHIN' OVER PORTA-CANS AT THE 4H RODEO

SINCE THEN THEY DANCED THERE LITTLE DANCE
JUST OUTSIDE THE LAW .
POPPED TWICE IN OKLAHOMA AND ONCE IN ARKANSAS
I DON'T KNOW WHAT POSSESSED ME TO WANTA TAG ALONG
CAUSE I'D BEEN RAISED A CHRISTIAN I KNEW RIGHT FROM WRONG

RIGHT OR WRONG BLACK OR WHITE
CROSS THE LINE YOUR GONNA PAY
IM THE DAWN BEFORE THE LIGHT
LIVE OR DIE BY SHADES OF GRAY

WE STOLE TWO CHAROLETTE HEIFERS FROM RANDY'S SWEETHEARTS PA
SOLD THE AT THE SALE-BARN OUTSIDE OF WHICKITA
WE GOT NINE HUNDRED DOLLARS & NEVER DID SUSPECT
THE WORLD OF HURT WE BE IN ONCE WE CASHED THE CHECK

NEXT DAY WE HEARD
BUT THAT DAY THEY RAN THE STORY ON THE LOCAL RADIO
SCARED AS HELL THAT NIGHT WE PACKED & LEFT FOR MEXICO
AND I SWEAR WE WOULD HAVE MADE IT IF IT WASN'T FOR THE STATE
CAUSE I GOT SICK ABOUT THE TIME WE CROSSED THAT KANSAS LINE

CHORUS ———

I WAS LAYING IN THE BAR DITCH PRAYIN' I WOULD DIE
WHEN A FLASHLIGHT SHONE DOWN FROM UP ABOVE A VOICE CALLED FROM THE SKY
A HALF A DOZEN UNMARKED CARS CAME SCREECHIN' TO A HALT
~~BOB WAS POINTIN' AT ME CRYIN~~
~~I SAW BOB CRYIN' POINTIN'~~ IT WAS ALL MY FAULT
They grabbed Bob & he started screamin

THEY SMASHED BOB AGAINST THE ~~FEED~~ TRUCK THREW RANDY INTO THE BED
SOME ONE HAD ME BY THE HAIR A SHOTGUN TO MY HEAD
BOB JUST BROKE DOWN CRYIN' AND TOLD 'EM WHAT WE DONE
He COULDN'T KEEP FROM CRYIN' AND BLAMIN EVERYONE

~~PARDON~~ There Men & Dogs & helicopters buzzin all around
They had the Brothers on the Pickups hood
                              & me down on the ground
Bob just went to pieces But Randy he held tight
Then a black man in a suit & tie stepped   onto the light
                                    half drunk
They left us like they found in ~~broke~~ and alone
Randy got behind the wheel said I'm goin home
~~He left oklahoma ~~~~ in~~
~~we drove slowly back to Kansas.~~

~~August 1995 · The Sun shone up in Kansas.~~
~~was · late .~~ The Morning sun in Kansas then took a in fire
It was ~~in April~~ in April 1995
~~The morning sun shone on and on~~
               On the Oklahoma line

He told his me to turn us loose
So they put down their guns
He said these are just some no good kids
They aint the ones

So the left us by the roadside hungover and alone
~~Hungover and alone~~
Randy got behind the wheel said "Boys we goin home"
we turned around go see our fate down hearted but alive
On that mornin in mid april Oklahoma '85

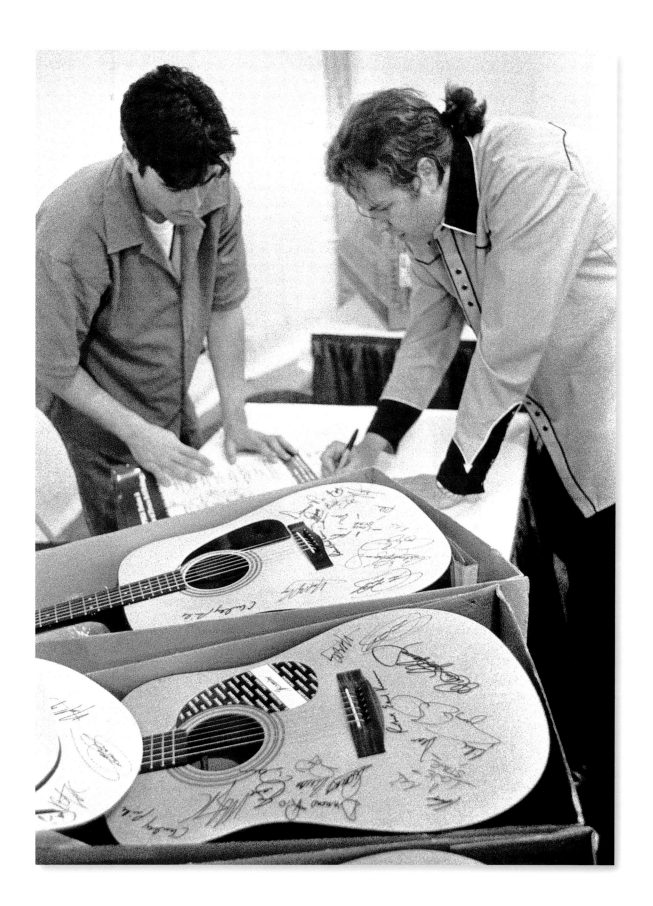

"Traditional."

WALKIN' CANE

Gravitational Forces | 2001

WALKIN' CANE

I got high and I got in jail.
I got high and I got in jail.
I got high and I got in jail.
Weren't nobody to pay my bail.
My sins they have overtaken me.

CHORUS

Hand me down my walkin' cane.
Hand me down my walkin' cane.
Hand me down my walkin' cane,
I'm a gonna leave on the mornin' train.
My sins they have overtaken me.

If I die in Tennessee,
If I die in Tennessee,
If I die in Tennessee
Ship me back by C.O.D.
My sins, they have overtaken me.

CHORUS

Hand me down my bottle of corn.
Hand me down my bottle of corn.
Hand me down my bottle of corn,
I'm gonna get drunk as sure as you're born.

CHORUS (3X)

"Someone on the website said,
this song is about World War II.
What a genius!"

MR. WOLF AND MAMABEAR
What I Really Mean | 2005

Things	**REK**
❶ Write a song	
❷ Work on book	
❸ Make a difficult decision	●
❹ Play guitar, mandolin, bass	◆
❺ Read a book to girls	●
❻ Exercise	◆
❼ Play chess	●
❽ Call a friend	●
❾ Organize something	◆
❿ Watch sunrise/sunset	●
New Things	
❶ Inspection # FOR TRUCK	◆
❷ CW Meeting –	
❸	●
❹	◆
❺	●
❻	●
❼	◆

MR. WOLF AND MAMABEAR

Mr. Wolf and Mamabear were
Banging on the door.
I told 'em once, I told 'em twice,
Don't come around here no more.
They've stolen all our Chickens,
They killed our neighbor's cat,
Last night I saw 'em talkin' to
Big Weasel and his rat.
It's such a cozy neighborhood,
We love our little town.
Lately things ain't been so good.
There's something goin' down.

It happened just a year ago,
Someone hired a band.
They had a dog and pony show
That got clean outta hand.
There was fur and feathers
Flying, the son of the old goat
Said Coon-Boy pulled a shotgun
From his worn out overcoat.
Bobcat killed Miss Peacock,
Coon-Boy shot the Mare,
While Mr. Wolf smoked opium
And grinned at Mama Bear.
Two dead ducks lay there
Beside Miss Peacock on the floor.
The fat Goose grabbed the
Telephone and called the Dogs of War.
The Guineas begged for
Mercy, the Pigs began to squeal;
Coon-Boy took the Kiddy,
Jumped in his automobile.
Bobcat and the Wheel Man,
The famous Wolverine,
Shot out the light and in the
Night they faded from the scene.

→

Chief detective Rambeauay
Did not work for free
And Sheriff Hog was called
Away unexpectedly.
The sheriff's re-election,
The murder of the Mare
Might get Hog implicated with
The Wolf and Mama bear,
So Rambeauay took up the case
Then shut it down for good.
He bought a house in southern France
But lives in Hollywood.

The bodies of the Bobcat and
The famous Wolverine
Were found inside a motel
Room outside of San Juaquin.
The city council voted the
Insurance board to pay
The victims of that heinous
Crime upon that dreadful day,
And I watch from the shadows where,
Beneath a frosty moon,
Mr. Wolf and Mama bear
Feed on a dead raccoon.

"It's all about Rich's guitar."

GOIN' NOWHERE BLUES
Gravitational Forces | 2001

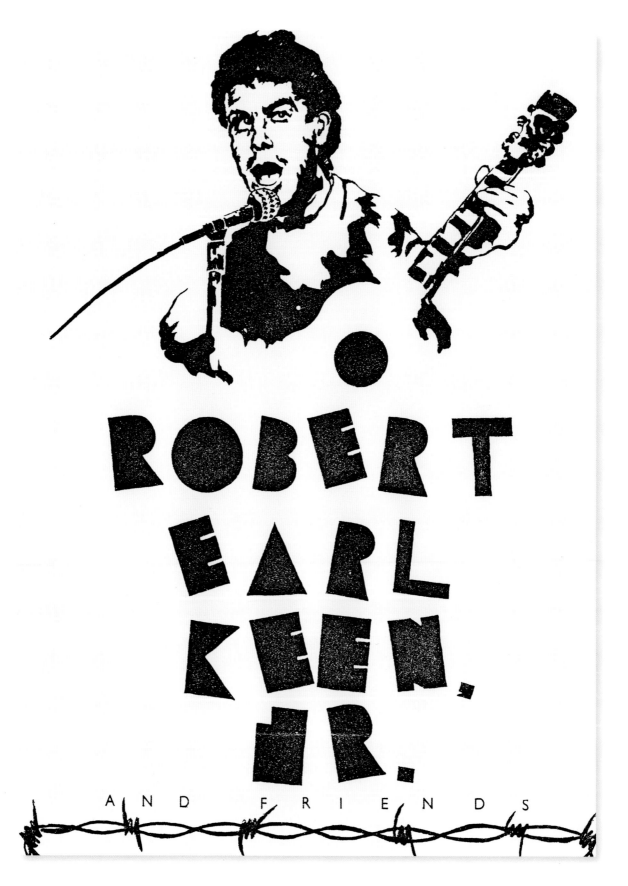

GOIN' NOWHERE BLUES

In the corner of the barroom
Lives the ghost of Langston Hughes
He's takin' notes and smokin' cigarettes,
Sippin' slowly on his booze.
Got them goin' nowhere blues.

And on the stage beneath the spotlight,
Woody Guthrie sings the news.
He's always ready for the good fight,
Never thinkin' that he'll lose.
Got them goin' nowhere blues.

Through the back way in the alley,
Sellin' all you should refuse,
Looks like Jane has finally given in.
Hey, what the hell it ain't no use.
Got them goin' nowhere blues.

Out the front around the corner
Martin Luther shines your shoes.
He's preachin' justice and equality.
I guess Martin's payin' dues.
He's got them goin' nowhere blues.

BRIDGE

On the other side it's a free ride.
You've got money you can burn.
When the ground shakes and the earth breaks
Which way you gonna turn?
Are you ever gonna learn?

In the poolroom on the table
Swillin' wine and smashin' cues,
They locked him up last night for fighting.
Cesar Chavez blew a fuse.
He's got them goin' nowhere blues.

All the members of the union,
All the farm and labor crews,
They used to meet here by the dozens;
They disappeared in ones and twos.
Got them goin' nowhere blues.

So you wonder why they come here.
They come here to look for clues.
Passin' time until they live again,
To fight these goin' nowhere views.
Leave these goin' nowhere blues.
To fight these goin' nowhere views.

"Nothing else matters."

LET THE MUSIC PLAY
Farm Fresh Onions | 2003

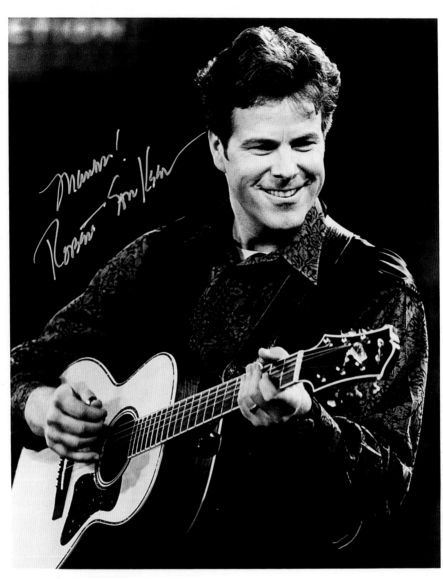

Photo: Scott Newton

Robert Earl Keen

 59 Music Square West
Nashville, TN 37203

615 327-4646
615 327-4949 FAX

```
  I          4             I
PUT THE HORSE IN THE STABLE
  #4        #
LOAD THE MULES ON THE TRAIN
        I          4              I
Set PLACE YOUR PISTOLS ON THE TABLE
     5        4          I
LEAVE THE DOGS IN THE RAIN


TAKE THE MONEY THEY GAVE YOU

HIDE IT IN A JAR

NOBODY NOW CAN SAVE YOU

DON'T MATTER WHERE YOU ARE

       4
   TURN YOUR LAMP DOWN LOW
       5
   HEAR THE FOUR WINDS BLOW
       I      to        6M
   BOW YOUR HEAD TO PRAY
       WASN'T WHAT YOU PLANNED
   3m              6M        4         5       I    4 I 4
   YOU GOT ONE LAST STAND)  LET THE MUSIC PLAY

LEFT FOR DEAD IN GEORGIA

AT THE HANDS OF SAD EYED JOHN

(WITH) YOUR  BABY  CALLIN FOR YA

YOU WERE HOME BEFORE THE DAWN


("YOU KNOW) OR (YEAH) YOU'RE SHAKEN HANDS WITH SATIN

YOUR MOUTH IS GOIN DRY
                    BACK IN
WHEN THAT LAWMAN FROM DAYTON

WON'T LOOK YOU IN THE EYE
```

He WAS NOTHIN BUT A
~~THEN THERE WAS THE~~ GRIFTER
HE CAME TO PLAY THE PART
DISGUISED AS LUKE THE DRIFTER
TALK ABOUT ~~YOUR~~ A CHEATIN HEART

HE SOLD YOU DOWN THE RIVER
WHEN HE RODE INTO YOUR TOWN
THEN THAT SAME OL' INDIAN GIVER
STRUCK MATCH AND BURNED IT DOWN

CHORUS

NOW YOU'RE ALONE AND BARELY BREATHEN
LOOKIN DOWN FROM ABOVE
NEEDIN' SOMETHING TO BELIEVE IN
WANTIN' ONLY TRUTH & LOVE

THE STORM IS SLOWLY DYIN'
AT THE BREAKIN OF THE DAY
ALL THE STEEL GUITARS ARE CRYIN'
I'M ROLLIN DOWN THAT LOST HIGHWAY

CHORUS

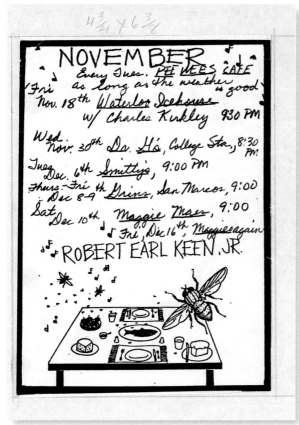

"I'm a stumbler."

DOWN THAT DUSTY TRAIL
Walking Distance | 1998

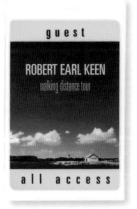
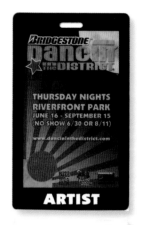

DOWN THAT DUSTY TRAIL

When I was a young boy,
The only things that really mattered
Were makin' friends and havin' fun.
Walkin' down the railroad track,
'Til you reached the river,
Turn around and head on back
When the day is done.

CHORUS

Ain't it like they always say,
Everybody goes their own way;
Nobody knows, no one can tell.
It's always been the same for me,
Guess it's just the way it must be
Headin' down that dusty trail.

When I was a young man,
The only things that got me goin'
Were gettin' high and chasin' love.
Lyin' down beside my girl
On the banks of the river,
With nothin' but some mustang
Wine and all the stars above.

CHORUS

It's a twistin' turnin' windin' road.
I get lost and broken down.
I'm a stumbler and it won't be long,
'Til i stumble back around.

Since I became my own man,
Everything that matters to me
Is makin' sure I'm stayin' true
To my friends and the ones I love
'Til I cross that river.
All alone I'm movin' on
Until my time is through.

CHORUS

"Post 9/11–The Narrator is a
cursed man who walks the earth
in order to exorcise his demons.
He doesn't recommend it."

BEATS THE DEVIL

Farm Fresh Onions | 2003

Beats the Devil Out of Me / Scorched

I can't remember when I was here but I'm back again
I barely know you friend but everything has changed
The sun burned up and the sky turned green
The air it smelled of gasoline
The soldier boy and the teenage queen
Have ~~been~~ since become estranged

Mmmm I keep moving
Like the wind on the sea (Like the wind across the sea)
          what you?
Mmmm   What I'm doin
Beats the devil out of me

I was tethered to the plow
Came untied I don't know how
That's all behind me how
Like some exotic dream
I woke up in oil and mud
Sticks & stones and bones and blood
~~Every~~ Everything I knew was good
Had vanished with the steam

Chorus

Now I walk this earth to find a place to rest some piece o'mind
~~And~~ I'll keep on until I'm blind or til' I'm old and gray
And so my friend good luck to you
I wish you well in all you do
Here's hopin' that your dreams come true
~~Y~~ AND may you never say ...   (And you never have to say)
                                    (And you won't have to say)

Chorus

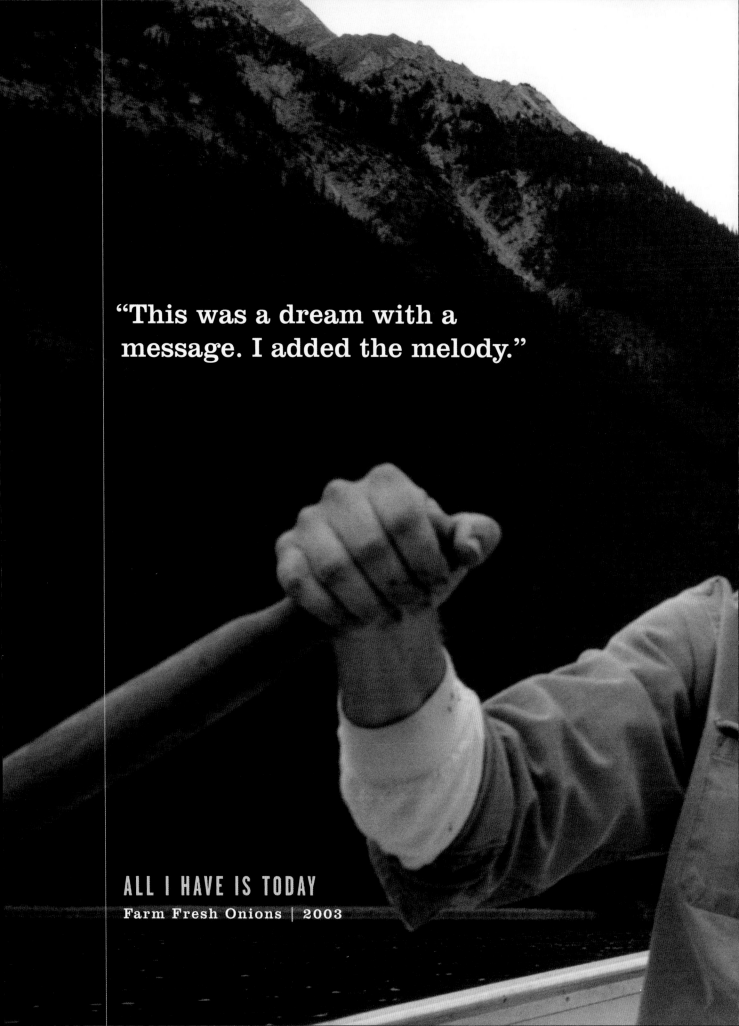

"This was a dream with a message. I added the melody."

ALL I HAVE IS TODAY
Farm Fresh Onions | 2003

After 12 years, Robert Earl Keen Jr.'s music has finally began to earn some recognition.

Entertainment

Fellow artists help convince Keen to accept own talent as songwriter

Continued From Page One

'My Last Duchess' by some 19th century poet (Robert Browning). That poem describes this picture of a woman, and later you find out that the guy describing it had killed her. It's a great poem. You start off from the outside looking in, then you understand the characters once you get on the inside."

Keen added that he prefers being known as a performer rather than a songwriter, but there are times when other artists force him to accept his own talent. "I have grown a lot more confident. That's true. When I first heard Joe Ely's recording of 'Whenever Kindness Falls,' I remember thinking to myself, 'That's so cool. I wrote that.'"

His serious songs do give way on occasion to humor on stage, but he's writing fewer funny songs for fear of being labeled incorrectly. "I want people to be entertained," he said, "and nothing bores me more than some self-righteous folk singer who has nothing to say but wants to provoke some dark reaction philosophically. So I find that humor works best for me.

"I like to goof around – sort of like (Steve) Fromholtz. He could

have been a comedian if he just dropped the guitar and got a little more goofy. But I'm no comedian."

That point should become crystal clear when his fourth album is released in mid-February. "There's no comedy on it at all," Keen noted. "It's extremely narrative. Just story song after story song, but some of the best stuff I've ever written."

And guess what? It was recorded in, of all places, Nashville.

Keen evidently has buried his demons, continuing to record in the city that once bred depression. The 1993 release will feature guest appearances by Marty Stuart on mandolin and vocalist Maura O'Connell. For that matter, Keen revealed that his booking agent is in Nashville, he writes for a Nashville publishing

company – and he even rents an apartment in Nashville.

Not surprisingly, he just laughs when asked if he's forgiven Earle for convincing him to move to Tennessee back in 1985.

But at least Keen finally is paying the bills with his music, which is more than his father ever expected. "Dad's standard line to me was always, 'Son, I think music's a great avocation. But I'm not sure it should be your vocation.' So to appease dad and mom, I always had other jobs.

"But I haven't had a real job since January of 1987 when I was working at a bookstore at Vanderbilt. My music seems to be working out just fine now.

"And I really couldn't be happier."

	2006	January		2007	February		2007	March		2007	
W T F S		S M T W T F S			S M T W T F S			S M T W T F S			

Tuesday November 14

318/47

this is from *Cities of the Plain* by Cormac McCarthy   pg 192/93

"He knew that those things we most desire to hold in our hearts are often taken from us while that which we would put away seems often by that very wish to become endowed with unsuspected powers of endurance"

pg 97 "every act which has no heart will be found out in the end. Every gesture."

Messages

Picture to house

ALL I HAVE IS TODAY

I woke up in another strange place
By a forty acre parking lot with every kind of sign.
I was talking to another strange face
Who was telling me it didn't have the time.

CHORUS

All I want is behind that mountain;
All I need is the other way;
All I am is a lost soul searching;
All I have is today.

I was walking through the sands of silver
To the sapphire canyon on the river of jade.
I was following a golden sun setting
When suddenly the light began to fade.

CHORUS

I was riding in a black Tornado
With the top pulled down and the lights on dim.
I heard angels singing in the darkness,
Singing some southern gospel hymn.

CHORUS

I was thinking 'bout a man and woman
Who were trying to make a living out of shiny wood and steel.
I should tell you if I haven't told you, this is exactly how I feel.

CHORUS

CHORUS

POST
TELEGRA

TELEGRAPH STORE

ICE

"Who the hell knows when Phoenix stops and Scottsdale begins. God Bless Uncle Joe!"

FURNACE FAN

Farm Fresh Onions | 2003

album reviews

By LOUIS HILGARTNER
Staff Reviewer
Rush
Grace Under Pressure
PolyGram
★★★

Robert Earl Keen
No Kinda Dancer
Workshop Records
★★★★

Robert Earl Keen has several things going for him.

Besides being an Aggie and having a backup band called **Some Other Guys**, which features dobro guitarist Ron Huckabee, Keen is a gifted songwriter with a talent for painting pictures with his lyrics.

That his voice is similar to Jerry Jeff Walker's is irrelevant; the heart of the matter is his songwriting.

Keen can take you to an old dance hall on a summer night, sing a real tearjerker or bring back memories of a lost love.

Probably the highlight of *No Kinda Dancer* is the "novelty" song "Swervin In My Lane."

Sung in the most traditional, corn-poney, country voice imaginable, Keen somehow draws a perfect analogy between the girlfriend that did him dirty and that damn drunk driver that keeps running him off the road.

Robert says he wants to become rich and famous.

He's definitely starting off on the right foot.

Pat Travers
Hot Shot
PolyGram
★★

Cover: What do you do with a B.A. in English from Texas A&M? If you're Robert Keen, you move to Austin, start writing songs and knock on a lot of doors. Along the way, you win the 1983 Kerrville New Folk Songwriting Award and cut an album. Keen is featured on this week's cover mostly because he's an Aggie and can make the right contacts. He also writes pretty decent songs. Photo by Bill Hughes.

FURNACE FAN

We were at the Rhythm Room in Scottsdale, Arizona.
It was in the summertime, it must have been '02.
We got there way too early and we sat around for hours.
We loaded in when the man came down and the Smushball game was through.

You can fry an egg out there on the city sidewalk.
You can fry your bacon and and and and and
And I understand why lizards live in sunny Arizona.
Why people do and call it home I'll never understand.

CHORUS

It's hotter than a furnace fan out in Arizona.
A hundred 'n ten ain't nothin' when you live out there, you see.
Stars come out, they scream and shout, "Hey it's good to know you."
If you're going there and you don't mind, say hello for me.
If you're going there and you don't mind, say hello for me.

CHORUS

Uncle Joe, he lives out there in Phoenix, Arizona.
He wears a cap that spells it out, "Hi, I'm Uncle Joe."
His kid is in the restaurant biz so he brought us fourteen boxes
Of chicken strips and ranch style dip and wings from Buffalo.

CHORUS

The room was small but the crowd turned out in Scottsdale, Arizona.
They listened to the stuff we played and sometimes sang along.
We finished up but they wanted more so we kept right on playing.
We played and stayed in the desert shade 'til we played up every song.

CHORUS

If you're going there and you don't mind, say hello for me.

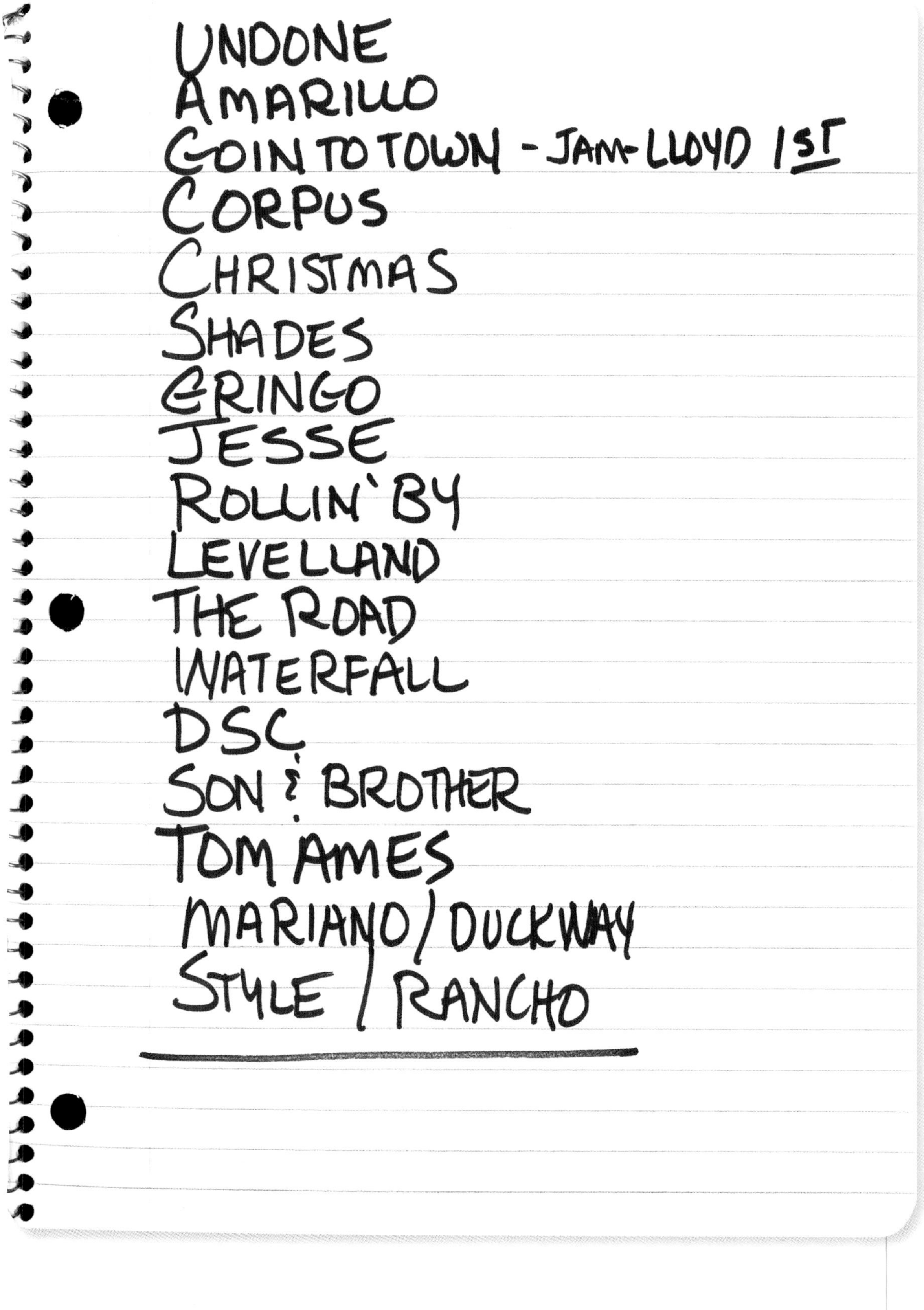

UNDONE
AMARILLO
GOIN TO TOWN - JAM- LLOYD 1ST
CORPUS
CHRISTMAS
SHADES
GRINGO
JESSE
ROLLIN` BY
LEVELLAND
THE ROAD
WATERFALL
DSC
SON & BROTHER
TOM AMES
MARIANO/DUCKWAY
STYLE / RANCHO

"Outlaw love."

FOR LOVE
What I Really Mean | 2005

FOR LOVE

Strapped my guns and courage on,
Set my cattle free.
Rolled a smoke and I made a vow
No more to be reviled.
Combed her hair and laid her out
Pretty as you please.
Watched the fire light up the night,
Crying like a child.

Saw a man in San Antone shoot
Down a dancin' queen,
And asked him on his hangin' day
What he was thinkin' of.
He said, "I never liked the way she
Treated me so mean.
In the end I tell you friend,
I did it all for love."

CHORUS

Stood out on the ragged edge and
There I took the fall.
I did it all for love, my friend. For
Love I did it all.

Just this side of Devil's Dream
Above the sulphur mine
I found the man who robbed me of
The girl I loved and lost.
I asked him before he died
What made him cross the line.
He asked me did I mean the line
That I just stepped across.

CHORUS

BRIDGE

Aghhhh Wonder Why?

I've walked this earth these many years
And left a trail of fire.
But once I was a gentleman,
Every bit like you.
Watched the heavens open up,
Heard the angel choir
Sing the hold song of God,
To thine own self be true.

"Amen."

THE ROAD GOES ON FOREVER
West Textures | 1989

THE ROAD GOES ON FOREVER

Sherry was a waitress at the only joint in town
She had a reputation as a girl who'd been around
On Main Street after midnight, a brand new pack of cigs
A fresh one hanging from her lips, a beer between her legs
She'd ride down to the river and meet with all her friends
The road goes on forever and the party never ends

Sonny was a loner, he was older than the rest
He was going in the Navy but he couldn't pass the test
So he hung around town, he sold a little pot
The law caught wind of Sonny, one day he got caught
But he was back in business, they set him free again
The road goes on forever and the party never ends

Sonny's playin' eightball at the joint where Sherry works
When some drunken' out-of-towner puts his hand up Sherry's skirt
Sonny took his pool cue, laid the drunk out on the floor
Stuffin' a dollar in a tip jar, walked on out the door
She's runnin' right behind him, reachin' for his hand
The road goes on forever and the party never ends

They jumped into his pickup, Sonny jammed her down in gear
Sonny looked at Sherry said, "lets get on out of here"
The stars were high above 'em, the moon was in the east
The sun was settin' on 'em when they reached Miami Beach
They got a motel by the water, a quart of Bombay Gin
The road goes on forever and the party never ends

They soon ran out of money but Sonny knew a man
Who knew some Cuban refugees that delt in contraband
Sonny met the Cubans in a house just off the route
With a briefcase full of money and a pistol in his boot
The cards were on the table when the law came bustin' in
The road goes on forever and the party never ends

The Cubans grabbed the goodies and Sonny grabbed the jack
He broke a bathroom window and climbed out the back
Sherry drove the pickup through the alley on the side
Where a lawman tackled Sonny and was readin' him his rights
She stepped in the alley with a single shot .410
The road goes on forever and the party never ends

They left the lawman lyin' and they made their getaway
Got back to the motel just before the break of day
Sonny gave her all the money, he blew her a kiss
"If they ask you how this happened say I forced you into this"
She watched him as his taillights disappeared around the bend
The road goes on forever and the party never ends

Its Main Street after midnight just like it was before
Twenty-one months later at the local grocery store
Sherry buys a paper and a cold six-pack of beer
The headlines read that Sonny is goin' to the chair
She pulls back onto Main Street in her new Mercedes-Benz
The road goes on forever and the party never ends

Endless Highways

ROBERT EARL KEEN: "My heart is really in performing. I like to see people enjoy the music and have a good time."

Keen goes again to where his audiences are – on the road

By Ed Bumgardner 8049T
JOURNAL ARTS REPORTER

■ **ROBERT EARL KEEN** *will perform at 9 p.m. Wednesday at Ziggy's. Admission is $10. Tickets: 748-0810.*

In the time-capsule cow-town of Bandera, Texas — where working cowboys still ride horses downtown — the only resident who *doesn't* wear a cowboy hat is the town's resident country singer and songwriter.

"Nope, I don't wear the hat —

but the residents overlook it and let me live there anyway," said Robert Earl Keen. "Bandera is a wonderful, magical place. I carry it with me wherever I go.

"For instance, right now, I'm physically in Ann Arbor, Mich., but my heart and mind are actually in Bandera. Amazing, isn't it?"

Homesick heart and wayward mind withstanding, Keen, his luggage and his band recently left Bandera and hit the highway after a three-month break from performing. It

was the habitually touring Keen's longest respite from the road since 1984, the year he released *No. Kinda Dancer*, the first of six critically acclaimed albums.

Keen's much-anticipated vacation did not turn out quite as envisioned.

"I had scheduled all this wonderful stuff to do at home," Keen said. "I came off the road . . . and immediately got this weird flu that kept me in bed for nearly two months."

See KEEN'S MUSIC, Page D7

These lyrics and this music
are dedicated to the
memory of Larry Brown.

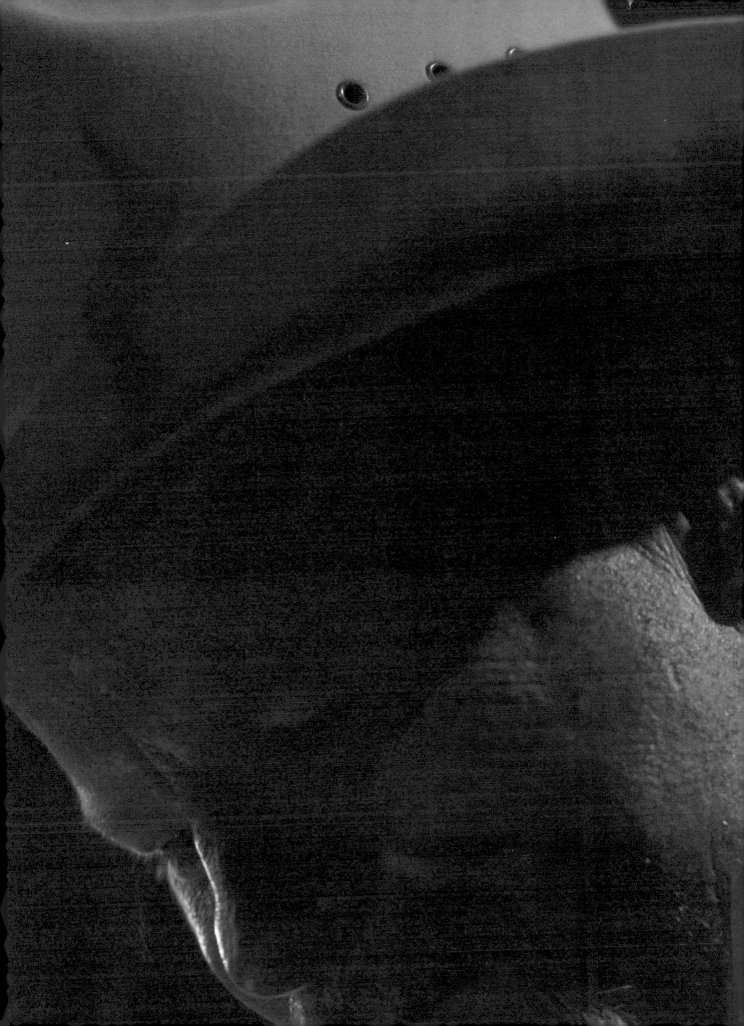